Memory Seeds

For Babs,
Hope you enjoy my poems
& Lesley's illustrations.
Jackie
x

about

The poet

Jackie Williamson is a retired journalist with a life-long
compulsion to write. She published her first full length book, a
sailing narrative entitled *Cevamp, Mike and Me* in November
2007 and her work appears regularly in a variety of magazines.
A prize-winning writer, she has contributed to two anthologies:
Banbury, published by Ottakar's in 2001 as part of their local
history series and *In Her Element*, published by Honno, the
Welsh Women's Press, in 2008. Describing her poems as more
doggerel than poetry, Jackie is currently working on a family
centred biography and a sequel to *Cevamp*.

Praise for Jackie's work

'A well written and good read.' *Self Publishing Magazine*
'Detailed, articulate and involving.' *Welsh Books Council*
'A wonderful read.' *Jamie Owen, BBC presenter and author*

The artist

Lesley Hall-Wood is a self taught artist. During her working life
as a funeral director she became involved in the designing of
memorial headstones. Since taking early retirement she has
experimented in various media. A few years living on the coast
in Cornwall resulted in marine based paintings, seascapes and
collages from beachcombings. Now living in Somerset, her work
reflects the local landscape and the flora and fauna of The
Levels in her highly detailed pen and ink drawings. Her work
may be found in galleries across the south west.

Praise for Lesley's work

'Lesley Hall-Wood's illustrations are both charming and
atmospheric. She has an ability to draw out the character of the
subject in her work, giving life to her drawings in a quality
which is unusual. Her choice of subject matter is often
evocative and always popular. Lesley's observations of rural life
transpose into beautiful, detailed illustrations.' *Vickie Hobbs,
Somerset Arts Week*

Memory Seeds

A collection of poems, rhymes and nonsense

Jackie Williamson

Illustrations by Lesley Hall-Wood

Acorns Publishing

Published in 2009
by Acorns Publishing

A catalogue record for this book is available from the British Library

ISBN 978–0–9557375–3–4

Designed and set by Elaine Sharples
St Dogmaels, Pembrokeshire
Tel: 01239 613338

Printed and bound by CPI Antony Rowe, Chippenham and Eastbourne

Acorns Publishing
Pembrokeshire

www.acornspublishing.co.uk
email acorns@acornspublishing.co.uk

This book is dedicated to our granddaughters, Rose and Harriet, who were born on the same day in different hemispheres, 19th December 2007.

the poems

that's life

Dylan Thomas

Oh Dylan Thomas I wish you'd lived to reach the year 09
then I could have read your poems
and you could have read mine.
We could have shared our feedback,
told each other what we thought
and learned from what each other wrote – would mine have
    come to naught?

Your choice of words are lyrical, the sounds so, so sublime
while I am struggling with the flow
and strive to find a rhyme.
What is this thing called meter?
What do they mean by scan?
And as for rhyming patterns – I need your guiding hand.

If you were here I'd follow you, blindly to the shore
and up the creaking wooden steps
and through your boathouse door.
I'd share your inspiration, you'd share my bright ideas,
we'd learn from one another and
we'd scorn each other's fears.

The fears that what we'd written wasn't good enough by half
or worse, that folk would think us mad
or worse still that they'd laugh.
'Who do they think they are?' they'd groan
and scowl and shake their heads.
Our fragile ego would be blown
like scattered silken threads.

But wait, I think I've got it wrong, it's odious to compare
your poetry with what I write –
just doggerel, to be fair.
But still I'd follow just to breathe the air that you exhale
and by osmosis I'd soak up
your genius, couldn't fail.

Where did you learn those golden words, the assonance so
   pure?
Your life spanned less than forty years
but still your works endure.
I know that after I am gone
and fifty years have passed
my words will be all but forgot –
I know they will not last.

Gidappy

I never read a book, I think,
until the age of four, then
my cousin gave me Gidappy –
we read it on the floor.

A new-born foal with legs so long
and eyes of limpid pools,
he started life so full of joy –
he didn't know the rules.
He walked into a spider's web,
the babies all fell out.
The mother spider scuttled forth:
'O Gidappy, you lout.'

Poor Gidappy, he hung his head
and left, at her command
but to his shame he trampled on
the local insect band.
The pictures were enchanting,
the words were big and round,
the pages large and colourful –
they made a creaking sound.

Thanks to this foal's adventures,
I soon began to know
that books are somewhere magical –
a special place to go.

Mobile library

Across the fields, above the
  hedges
manoeuvring round
the bends in the lane
you can just see the roof of
  the library van –
time to change our books
  again.

We wait in the lay-by, the
  lorry reverses
with grinding gears and
  annoying beep-beep.
We talk local gossip,
discuss all our ailments
then painfully clamber the
  steps –
they're so steep.

We hand our books over, all
  chattering brightly
of authors and titles and holidays and stuff;
we search through the volumes
packed tightly on shelving
to find something new, and well written –
not tough.

Our choices are date-stamped,
  we say our farewells,
the librarian closes
the door with a heave.
Then we all go our own way,
our books weighing heavy,
the gathering is over, we're ready
to leave.

The diet
On the first day of my diet it was actually tomorrow.
Ask any woman if you don't know what that means.
You're fat, unlovely, skirts too tight, knickers up your you know
  where
and you yearn to be the figment of some fashionista's dreams.
So you scoop more peanut butter from some dark clandestine
  store
and read your growing pile of magic, weight loss magazines
and reach out for that sneaky pot of Pringles, just one more and
vow tomorrow will be different.
That's when you'll start the diet.

So on the first day of the diet I started really well:
refused all offered pastries, croissants, choc and sweets and
  bread
and dined on fat free flat fish, steamed bland, with mushy
  swede
and for pudding turned down cheesecake, had dried apricots
  instead.
By bedtime I was starving – but had one thought in my mind
that in the morning I'd be sylph like. Even though I felt half
  dead
it'd be worthwhile tomorrow, for on the scales I'd find
I'd dropped at least a dress size
and shed a good half stone.

Woke up today, leapt out of bed and went and had a wee,
then stripped and only then dared stand upon the scale.
When I looked down to read the dial, my smile turned to a
  frown
how can this be, this can't be right, I'm heavier than a whale.
I'm two pounds more than what I weighed before I went to bed –
still floppy, fat and frightful, round as rolled up hay in bales
and I wonder if it's worth my while to weight watch, not eat
  bread
if it doesn't make a difference
and my life is just the same.

Demon drink

Me? An alcoholic?
  Whatever do you
  mean?
The times when I am
  tempted are few
  and far between.
Oh thanks, make
  mine a G & T, and
  then I'm on my
  way.
What's that?
  Another? Line
  them up – I've had
  a rotten day

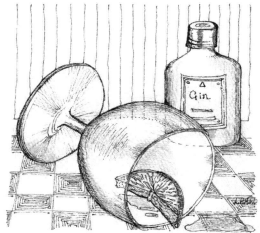

But alcoholic? No not
  me, I never touch the stuff
until, well, after breakfast, when I feel a little rough.
But alcoholic? Course I'm not, I never drink alone,
except when there is no-one in, and I am on my own.

I'm not an alcoholic. I go to work each day.
Okay, I'm sometimes rather late, when things don't go my way.
But I'm not an alcoholic: I've money, car and house
Except my ex kept all of them, the scheming, filthy louse.

I'm not an alcoholic. I've still got all my mates.
They're all around me, in this bar – we really get on great.
Out on the bevy every night, from happy hour, see,
then someone starts a punch-up and we go to A & E.

Call me an alcoholic? You must be raving mad.
I could easily give it up. But I am not THAT bad.
And I will get the next round in – you can think what you think
and if I'm sounding like a fool, well blame the demon drink!

Warning take two

When I am even older than I am today I'll
get my hair cut short again, let it gather grey
and shock, horror, worse than that, I'll
grow my armpits, and my legs and
let corns and bunions, rough scratchy skin,
adorn my feet.

And I will give up queuing; I'll just
hobble to the front and bang my stick and
say 'I'm an old aged pensioner. I've
paid my way. I shouldn't have to wait.
Young folks these days have no respect.
I blame the Welfare State.'

And then I will get into debt, abuse
my plastic, spend, spend spend on
anything I want or need – or don't – and
everything that takes my fancy then,
when bills roll in, make out I'm senile,
blame the lenders for their folly.

And when the sun shines, hot, enticing, I
will take my clothes off on the beach and
let it warm my skin and bones and turn
my wrinkles into leather and if people shy away,
say it's disgraceful, I won't even care.

And I will still watch the boat race with
lust and toothless leer at
all those fit young men and I
will still ponder on their stamina, imagine
how they'd look in just their boxers and their six packs
and that look needs no words.

Insomnia

Am I a lark or am I owl? It's really hard to say.
I don't think I am either – what comes out at mid-day?
Englishmen and mad dogs prefer the noon day sun:
that's when you'll find me waking up (or maybe not till one)!

The early dawn is lovely. I know because I see
the sleepy sun creep up the hills and search around for me.
But I am an insomniac, I lie awake all night
and just as dawn is breaking, sleep comes with morning light.

I wake for tea at eight o'clock, or earlier if dogs bark
and stagger down for porridge, then take them to the park.
But not a word I mutter till eleven, twelve or one,
and then I take my clothes off, and lie out in the sun.

By nightfall I'm exhausted, I have to go to bed.
I never hear the screech owl hoot, I sleep as though I'm dead.
But then at half-past midnight, I snort myself awake:
I think I've been asleep for hours but no, my slumber's fake.

I often wonder to myself what can the answer be?
Valerian or yoga, or hypnotherapy?
The only thing that knocks me out is really quite pathetic:
I'll have to go to hospital and have an anaesthetic!

Terribly shy

You know the sort of child I mean, I think,
lives in her own world, of books and dreams,
cries over dead birds, rescues lame ducks
longs to be liked, but thinks, it seems,
she never will.

Crippled by shyness, keeps her head down low,
then doesn't have to face rejection
if she says hello to mother's friend
who stares, and after some reflection,
says who are you?

Next time they meet, she makes a big pretence
of needing urgently to tie her shoes.
Keeps face averted until danger's passed
then goes on, happy with her ruse.
It worked, she's safe.

She has one friend; they met when they were five
first day at infants, held each other's hand
and stayed together till they reached their teens
and giggled over boys and made their plans
for wedding nights.

They said that they were really far too shy
to strip off all their clothes before their groom
and vowed they'd turn the lights off, or perhaps
hide in the wardrobe, make him leave the room
or not get wed.

Of course it didn't happen quite like that.
Hormones and swinging sixties came along
and getting married first became passé
and nakedness no longer seemed so wrong
Shy girl? Not she!

What I would like to lose ...
What I would like to lose would be
the letter O and the letter D.
They pop up far too regularly,
out there for all the world to see,
and prove to HIM I'm hopeless.

What I would like to lose, and quick,
is white and floppy, dense and thick.
It hangs, a shelf, above my knicks:
less VPL, more wet sponge bricks,
spare tyre spreads round my middle.

What I would like to lose, and fast
is guilt from actions in the past –
a mother's guilt, programmed to last,
that hits with an atomic blast
just when you least expect it.

What I would like to lose THIS week
are cobwebs, dog hairs, muddy feet
and things that stop me being neat
and tidy, make me feel dead beat,
this week that ends with Christmas.

What I would like to lose, it seems
can only happen in my dreams.
Fat Christmas money spiders teem
with guilt maternal, piled in reams,
for life goes on, regardless.

Riot

It's a riot of colour, my garden,
yet it's nothing to do with me.
I don't really know how it happened –
it's thanks to the bird and the bee.

The person before put some shrubs in,
some flowers, some grass AND some weeds
but where did the rest all appear from?
It's nothing to do with me.

My friend brought me plants from her border –
put them here, put them there, she decreed.
I did as she said, as she ordered
but the slugs and the frost came with speed.

The plants, once so pretty and cheerful,
just vanished without any trace.
I hoped that my friend wouldn't visit,
to see just a bare barren space.

But wait, just a year or so later
my border burst out into flames.
Don't ask me what plants are now thriving –
I'll never remember their names!

The sounds of thyme

The sounds of thyme, of blade on board,
of herbs chopped fine and small
are timeless, universal, the kitchen sounds of all.

From mud huts to grand palaces,
from tents to jungle floor,
the methods are all much the same, and always it's a chore.

But from these simple savoury plants,
a bit of veg and meat,
aromas waft, hang in the air, and make you want to eat.

Such simple food's a leveller
from here to Hindustan
it's what makes humans all the same, that strange old race
    called man.

Firstborn

I know it's a cliché, to call a
new born baby a cherub. But
you really were. Rosebud lips.
Dark fringed mahogany eyes.
A cap of pale auburn hair.
Soft, downy skin: peaches and
cream. More clichés. But
clichés are born of truth. They
say you forget the pain of
childbirth, once it's all over. In
labour you don't believe it's
true. But the first time I held
you, met your solemn gaze, all I could feel was a love so
overwhelming that it consumed every other feeling, every other
emotion. I knew I would never, could never, love this much again.

Grass

The grass is always greener on the far side of the fence.
I always want what I don't have – the feelings are intense.
When I go shopping for my clothes and take the garments home
I wish I'd bought the OTHER things – it really makes me
    moan.
When eating in a restaurant I cannot choose a dish
so I pick chicken, beef or pork then wish I'd chosen fish.
If asked what shall we do today I answer I don't care
but when we do the things HE wants, I think, this isn't fair.
Our skiing hols I'm sad to say were down to me this year –
there was no snow, we could not ski, so why did we come here?
Despite my best intentions, I guzzle wine or gin
then wish I hadn't done that, best intentions never win.
So what can be the answer, for making up my mind?
Or is it just my nature, a foible of mankind?

Perfect weekend

Saturday dawned misty
so we lazed around in bed –
we'd planned to go out walking,
but had a snooze instead.
At nine o'clock the sun burst through.
We had a change of plan:
'Come on, get up, get ready, the bus is due at ten.'
We drove the car to Fishguard, then bussed to Dinas Cross
and walked down to Pwllgwaellod –
the lie in was no loss.
The dogs thought it was heaven,
the views were just sublime;
the miles we walked were seven:
we had a lovely time.

On Sunday it was market day at the bleak airfield hall.
We took my mum, she bought some spuds, she didn't hear the
    call.
My sister rang to tell me that Ivor, my mum's pal,
had died the night before and
I'd be the one to tell.
We took Mum out for dinner and then we took her home.
'Bad news,' we said, 'It's Ivor.'
'Oh no,' she said, 'Who phoned?'
I really was quite worried; I thought she'd be upset.
But no, she seemed quite pleased to think
that she'd outlived him yet!

Maenchlochog

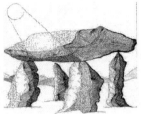

'Don't move to Wales,' was what they said.
All our family. And our friends.
'You'll hate it there. The Welsh don't like
the English.
They'll slag you off. They'll burn your
house.
And your cars. They'll hate you. You won't
be happy.
You'll be back. You'll see.'

We moved to Wales regardless
of what they thought and what they said.
We like it here. Feel we are liked. Our house still stands.
Our cars are safe. We are happy.
We put down roots, absorbed the culture. We have Welsh
    friends.
We won't be going back.

Mud on the roads? 'Who cares?' we say
and pressure-hose slurry off windows and walls,
sluice fox dung from our dogs and boots
and clamber up ladders to fix loose slates,
rattling in Pembrokeshire gales.

Slowly we absorb the secrets
and ancient mysteries of this old land, new home.
We learn the language – a bit – and speak
the place names with no vowels with pride.
Eglwyswrw? Easy!

'Where is Maenchlochog?' asked the man,
a stranger in a bar of locals.
We who knew exchanged glances, smiled.
Would we share this secret with a stranger?
English he was.
Strange to me now too.

Shit happens

'It's time to crane the boat out.
Autumn's here again.
The tide is high, the crane is booked,
I hope it doesn't rain.
Let's motor up on Sunday,
put her beside the wall,
then Monday morning we'll be there,
before the tide can fall.'
We climbed aboard on Sunday,
the ropes they were all set.
The tide was high, the wind it blew,
we knew that we'd get wet.
'Go and switch the batteries on,'
said Mike to me on deck.
I turned the key, he pressed the switch.
No engine. What the heck?
'Oh bugger,' said my captain,
'Oh hell, oh shit, oh fuck.
'We should have guessed about this.
'It's just our bloody luck.'
We took the battery home again
and put it on to charge;
then took it back down to the boat –
by now more like a barge.
We got it all connected,
I stood by husband's side.
It started up no problem,
but whoops, oh dear, no tide!

Fate

When I was in my teens I knew
what life for me had set in store.
I had exams to pass, that's true,
but fool I was, I wanted more:
job, freedom, love, engagement ring,
I knew would make my young heart sing.

I got my grades and got them well,
then boyfriend, job and money too.
Did I get freedom? Did I hell!
A shotgun wedding – nothing new.
Emancipation? Not for me –
just nineteen years of drudgery.

The children grew. Before I knew
they'd fledged the nest, and freedom called.
Husband and wife had grown up too,
the marriage dead, the flames grown cold.
This time I knew just what to do:
'Be strong, walk out, live life for you.'
I gathered threads of my career
and in a new life struck out, bold.
Job, freedom, self respect held dear –
no need of love, in search of gold!
I had my space, my wings to spread,
my friends, my work . . . my empty bed.

Then one March day Fate took a hand
and brought a new man to my life.
I wasn't looking, men were banned:
I had no wish to be a wife.
His eyes met mine, I heard bells ring,
I knew my heart would always sing.

I loved you once
How can I tell of memories of our love
when all I feel is dislike and frustration
and all I hear from you is whinge and moan?

By doing mundane tasks I shut you out
and dream of who I really want to be:
a person in my own right
with the spirit to break free.

I wonder what I ever saw in you;
or maybe I was fooled by love's young dream?
I yearn for romance, flowers and to be
cherished. But not by you.

Toy boy

Eyes brilliant with tears –
    or too much wine – you
    smile at him
across the bar.
He's young, you think, could
    be my son,
almost.
He meets your gaze, you
    think why not?
You're lonely, need some
    company,
tonight.

Don't need to justify your
    thoughts, not to yourself,
nor anyone.
Compassion, love, in short supply
for years.
You are the empty legacy
of marrying too soon, too young –
gone stale.

More wine, much more. You leave the bar and head for where?
You haven't said.
But you both know where this will lead.
Wine fuelled
you stumble at the door, go up,
embracing on the stairs
and tumble, molten, trembling
to the floor.

I love you, he says, when he can love you no more
and you feel the net
close in on you – you wanted less
than this.
You tell the truth, chapter and verse.
He doesn't understand. He weeps.
Goodbye.

Moving

The DI was a tough man, cockney born and bred:
he'd worked in inner cities, his heart ruled by his head.
But he was still compassionate, and not afraid to weep
in front of roughy toughy cops. His sympathies ran deep.
And this was shown quite clearly, one day in Milton Keynes
when police were called out on a shout, called by a group of
teens.
The kids had found a bundle, quite pale and still and small
lying beneath a hedgerow; it didn't move at all.
The DI went to take a look and moved the kids away.
He picked the thing up tenderly; the cops all heard him say
'Of all the jobs I've worked on, the places I have been,
this baby is the saddest thing that I have ever seen.'
He looked down at the bundle, the babe lay in his arm,
She did not move, she never had, this child would know no
harm.
Her mother was a child herself, with no-one she could tell.
She'd had her baby all alone, no-one could guess her hell.
She'd given birth then panicked; she needed to be found.
She wasn't very far away, was bleeding on the ground.
The DI stayed beside her. He held her while she cried.
And while her carers heard the news, he stayed right at her
side.

Posh

When I was little
my idea of posh
was a café where they gave you
hot buttered teacakes
and
hot water, in a silver jug,
to top up
the tea pot.

Lovers
Eyes meet, his lust rises; his love for the woman
comes later. He woos her with silver.
They talk, sharing laughter, shared pleasure in books
and drink wine on picnics, eat puddings of chocolate.
His fantasies of her in silken pyjamas
just harden his fancy – he will be her lover.

She looks, sleepy-eyed, at the face of her lover
and marvels how one night has turned girl to woman.
She sees on the floor crumpled silken pyjamas,
remembers the moonlight that cast shafts of silver
on bodies entwined, sweat sleek, sticky chocolate
and thought they don't tell you it's like this, in books.

Their mutual pleasures in love, wine and books
are the threads that connect them, from each to the lover.
She melts as he drowns in the dark pools of chocolate,
the mocha brown eyes in the face of his woman
as their old friend the moon bathes their romance in silver
and now she is naked, no need of pyjamas.

But time wreaks its havoc: 'Where are my pyjamas?
'I need them in bed while I'm reading my books.'
And 'don't buy me gold now my hair's turned to silver'
and 'I'd much rather cuddle my cat than a lover.'
The heartrending cry of the middle-aged woman
who's given up romance and only wants chocolate.

And life's so unfair for despite all the chocolate
his body's still firm, he's no need of pyjamas
and his fancy now wanders away from his woman.
He lusts after girls in the movies, and books
a date with a 'model', hopes she'll be his lover:
persuades her with baubles and charms her with silver.

But all is not lost, clouds have linings of silver:
the woman decided to give up the chocolate,
get thin, get a toy boy, a handsome young lover
and dress him in silk shirts and satin pyjamas
and teach him the joy of sex, not out of books,
but here, in the warmth of the thighs of a woman.

And guess what? The woman no longer wears silver.
She gave up her books, said goodbye to the chocolate
to live in pyjamas, and live for her lover.

Memory seeds

Now why did I just come upstairs?
Was it to stand and stare around
with vacant face and vacant mind?
I'd better go back down again,
do what it was I did before
to coax my brain to backward wind
and bring the memory to the fore.

I used to be articulate
and was never stuck for words
until I reached a certain age.
Mid-sentence now my brain goes blank.
What was it I was saying then,
before the words fell off the page
inside my head? The light's gone out.

I keep a notebook close to hand,
jot down the things I must recall,
like shopping, phone calls, where to go.
No sooner thought than write it down
before it goes. Now where's that pen?
I'm hunting for it, high and low
but memory fails me, yet again.

I wish that I could plant a seed
inside my brain, the memory
    bit,
to perk things up and make it
    spark
the way it used to years ago.
I'd startle people with my wit,
climb out of intellectual dark
once more into the light.

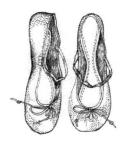

First dance

On points, pink satin,
shoes with a bow.
I'm four, a tomboy.
Ballet? Oh no.

'Okay, you win,
ballet no more.'
Red shoes, steel toes,
clack on the floor.

This time it's tap:
shuffle, hop, down.
Can't keep in step,
can't smile, only frown.

Ballroom comes next:
waltz two three, turn.
I trip, stumble, groan –
no, this I can't learn.

So come on let's twist,
let's rock and let's roll.
This is more like it,
this rhythm, this soul.

Brown eyed boy

I was a teenage momma
strugglin' by myself;
a babe in arms and a kid of three
and no food on the shelf.
Their daddy was a gamblin' man,
a drinker and a cheat
but I loved him for his dark brown eyes
with a love that was complete.

He wooed me with a band of gold
and promised we'd be wed
but the whiskey and the gambling meant
for me a lonely bed.
His loggin' wages all were spent
in bars or on a bet
and he ran up debts with Big Bad John
who carried out his threat.

My heart broke as I buried him,
to my kids I made a vow
that drink and gamblin' would not be
the way that we'd live now.
But still the bills came rolling in,
I had no way to pay;
out on the streets I would not go
I'd find a better way.

As I walked past the race course
one day with head down low,
I heard a gelding over there
a callin' me to go.
And as I looked right over
into his dark brown eyes
he seemed to say 'I'll help you
make up for all them lies'.

Could this be the answer,
to get me out of debt?
I walked right in, right there and then
and then I placed my bet –
put all my money on that horse,
my faith in his dark eyes
that seemed to burn into my soul
and promised me the prize.

They said his name was Brown Eyed Boy,
so young, so strong, so fine
and as he galloped round the course
his winnings would be mine.
He was leading by a head
as the final hurdle came
but he crashed down and broke his neck
and I cried out in pain.

The wagon came and took him in,
my tears they fell like rain;
I saw the vet man coming out
his gun was all too plain.
I turned away, I couldn't stay
the pain it hurt too much
and then I heard the shot ring out,
the dark brown eyes were shut.

Heard it on the news
I read it in the papers and I saw it on TV.
They said my baby's leaving, going far away from me.
I thought our love would be for keeps, forever and a day
but she's fallen for a movie star who's taking her away.

We met when we were seventeen, it only took a glance
to know she was the one for me, it was my first romance.
She promised me she would be mine and she would be my
    bride,
she said our hearts would be entwined and she'd stay by my
    side.

I read it in the papers and I saw it on TV.
They said my baby's getting wed; I guess it had to be.
For he can give her all the things that she could ever need
and he can give her diamonds – I only gave her beads.

But even so I wonder if she ever dreams of me;
no man could love her more than I, I dream she still loves me.
But he's a millionaire movie star, I drive a garbage cart
and he can give her what she wants I only have my heart.

Oh how I miss my baby, her smile, her voice, her eyes
Oh how I miss her soft perfume, her arms, her kiss, her sighs.
The nights are long and lonely now that she has gone away
She's run off with a movie star and I alone must stay.

nature in
the raw

Autumn

the nights they are a drawin' in
the wind it is a blowin'
the summer it has bin and gon'
and soon it will be snowin'

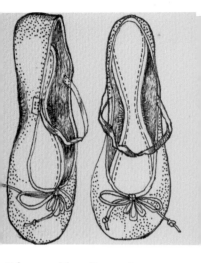

If you like Pam Ayres, you're bound to enjoy this collection of Jackie Williamson's rhymes and doggerel, inspired by the people and landscape around her North Pembrokeshire home.

Lesley Hall-Wood and Jackie Williamson have been friends all their adult lives. Their empathy and shared sense of humour shine through Lesley's magical illustrations of this collection.

memory
seeds

**a collection of poems
by jackie williamson
illustrated by
lesley hall-wood**

£5.95

Published by
Acorns Publishing
email:
acorns@acornspublishing.co.uk

ISBN 978-0-9557375-3-4

Bookmark design: John FA Wood

Evensong

The sad sweet song of the backdoor
  robin
fills this grey November day with colour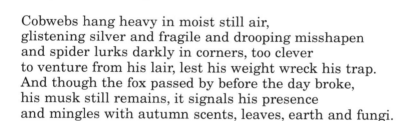
on a day when colour's thin on the
  ground
and just a few leaves hang on tight to
  the trees
and mushrooms and toadstools have
  mountains to break through
and only the campion turns its face skywards:
an optimist seeking the sun.

Cobwebs hang heavy in moist still air,
glistening silver and fragile and drooping misshapen
and spider lurks darkly in corners, too clever
to venture from his lair, lest his weight wreck his trap.
And though the fox passed by before the day broke,
his musk still remains, it signals his presence
and mingles with autumn scents, leaves, earth and fungi.

Though the red dragon droops, defeated, on flag poles
and washing hangs limp on the dew laden line
and it seems that the land is preparing to sleep,
life goes on. It's there in the soil of the newly tilled fields
where new shoots of young crops thrust out through the earth
and above the bare branches are great clouds of lapwing
and Jack Snipe flies zigzag from out of the scrub
and fieldfare and redwing seek snails on the ground.

And now as the sun starts to fire the horizon
a trilling crescendo of sound fills the world
it's evensong time from the choir in black feathers:
loud chatter from a thousand feathered throats.
as the starling tree singers strike up their finale
and fluff iridescent in evening's red glow
and press for position on bare twigs and branches.

Then stop.

Moonlight

Midsummer nights. The darkness
    creeps
with silent stealth; and though it
    seeps
through open panes it cannot
    match
the moonlight, shining on each
    patch
of bedroom floors, and pine and
    quilts
or on the mirror as it tilts
to catch the gleaming rays of light
that penetrate the shadowy night.
Outside the grass gleams olive, dew bright;
foxes hunt in night-long twilight.
Silent night is but a dream –
stark sounds of nature steal sleep's theme.

Porth Dinllaen

Last night I dreamt I went to
Porth Dinllaen again.
A horseshoe bay of sand and sun,
a place that sees no rain;
where Snowdon's mists roll out to sea,
where dolphins call and leap;
a place of refuge in a storm
where weary sailors sleep.
For Porth Dinllaen gives shelter
from seas that foam and roar:
a place of quiet refuge beside a Celtic shore.

Inhumanity

The woods are alive
with the sound of danger.
Wild creatures abound
though they can't be seen.
Dank mist fills the air,
hides the woodland ranger
and poachers all know
it's a night to be in.

The badger's abroad
roots for grubs in the
    darkness.
Quite harmless to man
but some men are his foe.
They fear for their herds,
blame the badger for sickness;
their traps are all set
but in truth they don't know.

And what of the fox
now that hunting's outlawed?
Free to roam at his will
he has nothing to fear.
But for hundreds of years
man has been his opponent
and get him he will –
if not hounds then by wheels.

So the woods are alive
in their own unique way.
They rustle and wail
sounds of life and of death.
So leave them in peace:
they don't have their own say.
Take care of them all,
let them be, give them breath.

Reflections on blue

Cathedral tranquillity, dappled light of green
with sunlight slanting through the canopy and
spotting the ground in lantern pools of gold.
Dense bluebell carpet fills the air with perfume:
sweet floral top-notes and dank, leaf mould damp.
Petals of windflowers, delicate as mayfly wings
curtsy in the breeze then flutter and bend,
reflected in the azure sky as soft white clouds
through tender May leaves, twigs and branches,
above.

Beyond the cool and dappled copse, reflections change
in the mellow, ripening heat of mid-day spring:
white clouds now liquid shadows, blue and grey,
chase waves and foaming ripples to the shore
while on the ragged cliffs, exposed to sun's full glare
squill lilies, soft pink thrift, bright gorse, soft mosses
form a tender rainbow pathway, fragile, hardy –
that's reflected in the corals deep
below.

Big spotties

The sun beat down, relentless.
Time passed.
The sky a cobalt canopy.
We waited.
The shimmering sea hid treasures
we watched for.
A turtle breached –
not him.
The morning passed
and still we waited.
Patient.
At last the cry went up:
'Big spotties,
below us.'
Not one, but two.
We jumped into the water
to see them,
be with them.
I wept.
Two whale sharks –
big spotties –
circling round beneath us.
Leviathans.
So rare.
Majestic.

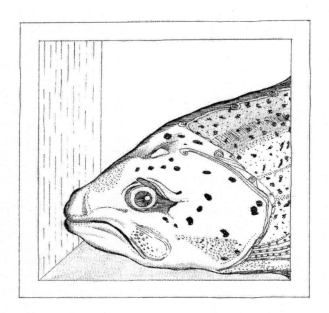

Give fish a chance

'Haddock, chips and peas' we cry, every Friday night
but little is the heed we give, to haddock and their plight.
A humble fish, and like the cod, its time is running out:
a favourite, simple dinner dish, in newsprint or without.

But Friday nights are changing now, the haddocks' course is
    run.
Big boats, long lines, wide open nets: the pot of gold is done.
We've fished our seas, no overfished, for far too long we know.
Now all that's left are little ones, no time for them to grow.

So what of Fridays? What to eat? With what to fill the space
left by the cod and haddock, the dogfish and the plaice?
It's time to get adventurous, to look for flavours new
so go down to the fishmonger and ask him what to do.
Look on his slabs, ask his advice and his opinion seek –
he'll tell you what to cook for tea this Friday, and next week.

Ground

The ground is a good place for burying things, such as treasure,
    time capsules . . . and pets;
it's the place where we put floating goldfish, and the creatures
    that die at the vets.

We started with Percy the tortoise, who from his deep slumber
    awoke
much too early, alas, one mild winter, and sadly, on lettuce, did
    choke.

Next came a striped kitten called Tiny, who learnt how to open
    the door
and liked to lie out on the road in the sun, but he doesn't do
    that any more.

The cavies fared better, lived life to the full, and produced little
    piglets so sweet;
but they run very quickly, grown ups failed to see when they
    sprinted right under
    their feet.

The dogs are the ones that
    hurt us the most – we
    wept as we dug out each
    plot;
they rest in the garden,
    three mounds in the
    grass, three sticks at
    their heads mark the
    spot.

And one far off day we will
    join them, our ashes all
    scattered around
and our spirits will float
    high above in the sky,
    our earthly remains in
    the ground.

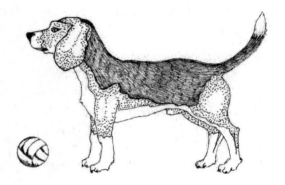

Harry
Nose to ground, deaf to all sound
until
two blasts on the whistle
get through.
Head up, muscles bunched,
he bounds
gazelle-like, graceful, swift
to me

stuff and
nonsense

Dragon lady

The dragon lady took the floor
with drum and tambourine,
red velvet dress and tousled hair
like none I'd ever seen.
You've heard the saying I am sure
that ignorance is bliss.
She should have asked us 'does my
    bum,
look very big in this?'
'Five minutes each,' the MC said
'we've no more time to spare'
but dragon lady took no heed
she didn't seem to care
that there were many poets there
who wanted to perform –
she just droned on, and on, and on
she didn't hear us yawn.
We waited for a moment's pause
to interrupt her flow:
we even raised our hands to clap –
she didn't want to know.
'Stand up and face the north,' she cried
'and listen to my song.'
Obediently we did as bid
and even sang along!
We turned to east, to south and west
And then sat down again
but had she finished? no you've guessed –
she really was a pain.
She spoke of dragon eggs that grow
and made the startling claim
that come next year, she has no doubt,
they will hatch out to reign.
She carried on in similar rote,
the minutes all ticked on.
Five? Ten? Fifteen? No – twenty three
then finally she was gone!

Monkeys on the roof
You should have heard the monkeys on the roof!
At first I thought this title was a spoof –
you don't get monkeys wild out here in Wales –
someone out there was telling fairy tales.

The noises in my roof are less exotic
and never, I should say, are they erotic.
They mainly come from wind and storms and squeaks
from mice and rats and starlings' tapping beaks.

And other natural causes, such as rain,
that sound like drumming on the window pane,
or howling gales that lift the roofing tiles –
and smash them into big expensive piles.

But monkeys? Never, to my certain knowledge.
Or maybe I should go right back to college?
How do you tell a monkey from a bird?
Or even from a rhyme like this?
Absurd!

Frog
A frog hopped out of the toilet.
It really made me jump.
It leapt out of the water
and bit me on the rump.

He jumped out of the toilet
and hit the ceiling fan.
I gathered up the pieces
and flushed them down the
pan.

To unblock all the pipework
it cost a hundred quid.
The moral of this tale is
always shut the lid!

Poo-belle

I am a lonely dog-poo bin,
bright red and in my prime,
standing proud upon my pole,
a beacon of our time.
You'll find me in a country park,
you'll find me in a town
and even when it's very dark
you can still track me down.
So what is my attraction?
It's very hard to tell
but day or night, winter or spring,
you'll find me by my smell.

Beware of the dog

'Beware of the dog' the big notice said,
nailed fast to the front of the fence;
but the visitor shrugged and just laughed it off,
'Dogs like me,' he said, 'sign's nonsense.'

He boldly marched forward and opened the gate,
the dobie rushed up all teeth bared.
The visitor gulped then he turned round and ran –
he really was feeling quite scared.

As he ran for the gate he tripped over some scrap,
the dobie gained ground, jumped
   and bit.
The visitor screamed, didn't know
   what to do
and then he went quiet. Oh shit.

The dobie was sated, all fury was
   spent,
his victim lay still on the floor.
The moral of this is always to pay
   heed
to the sign that is nailed to the door.

Three blind mice

There is a little nursery rhyme I learnt when I was three;
my mother taught it to me as I sat upon her knee.
You can sing along to it, the rhyming is quite nice
but like so many fairy tales, this tale of three blind mice
is gory, dark and worse than this, it tells of royal vice.

In sixteenth century England, big Henry was the King;
his first born child was Mary, a nasty little thing.
Her dad kept killing off his wives, he left the church behind
and Mary, Catholic through and through, could never be resigned
to give up Rome, pledge C of E, and change her holy mind.

When Henry died young Mary sat upon the throne as queen.
A woman monarch of the realm had not before been seen.
She married Catholic Phillip, a prince of Spanish blood
and earned the title farmer's wife: she did all that she could
to buy up pasture, farms and fields and even all the woods.

She wanted to build up her church, you couldn't disagree;
and if you did, off with your head, she punished heresy.
Archbishop Cramner, foolish, brave, abhorred the Church of
    Rome
and plotted with two noblemen to have her overthrown.
But Mary blew their cover; their followers gave a groan.

The three were soon convicted: burn at the stake she cried
and they were duly martyred; they prayed before they died.
But justice has a funny way of rearing up its head –
Queen Mary was a barren queen and once that she was dead,
Protestant Elizabeth ruled the land instead.

And so you see these nursery rhymes are not all they purport;
it wasn't quite a farmer's wife, it was a different sort
of murderous harridan in that rhyme, the head that bore the
    crown
and three blind mice were three good men who wouldn't be
    brought down
and Elizabeth was Good Queen Bess, her church is still around!

Naiad

A sunny day in early June, no different from the one before:
the sun beat down, the decks were hot, I didn't want to go
  ashore.
Straw-hat on head to shade my eyes from harsh and
  unforgiving glare,
I read my book, I dozed, I woke, nothing had changed, the rocks
  were bare.
Or were they? Something moved and I looked through the binos
  best to see
a pair of figures, outlined there, but faint and blurred, a mite
  hazy.
A man sat down. A girl emerged, her hair a halo in the light.
All dressed in black, she dragged behind a body board, not quite
  her height.
She bravely stepped into the sea and not a shiver shook her
  frame.
As waters lapped around her thighs I wondered, 'Is this girl
  insane?'
She slowly went in deeper still; she went up to her chest
and then, I swear, you won't believe, she danced her very best.
Arms up, arms down, she swam, she flounced, her element she
  had found.
I thought 'Is this a mermaid? or is her mind unsound?'
Or was I just imagining strange things I thought I'd seen
in heat and haze off Lampit steps? Or was it just Christine?

Strictly come dancing

Producer
"I've got to keep the ratings high
or they will axe the show.
If I can't cause some conflict then
I'll be the first to go.
I'd better wind the judges up
and make them cause a scene
and upset all the dancers
to keep the viewers keen."

Judges
"Don't be so nice, they said
    tonight,
please make your judgements
    vicious.
So we needled all the dancers
to gratify their wishes:
you're wooden, heavy-footed,
and you really have no flair.
Just keep on with the day job and
stay right out of our hair."

Dancers
"Last week our sizzling routines were
too hot for you to handle.
This week our foxtrot was sedate
but even now you wrangle.
I really think you've lost the plot,
you don't know your own mind.
Though we have practised hard and long
your words are still unkind."

Ode to the over-cooked Brussels sprout
Oh woe, alas, the knack I've lost of cooking a la dente.
I used to be so good at it but fear my talent's spent.
For hours I toil pre-Sunday lunch
with knife and sprout and gin
to cook the perfect weekend roast
on time, but oh, chagrin –
the meat is dry, the crackling soft, the Yorkshire pud's a biscuit.
I never seem to get it right, no matter how I whisk it.
And, oh no, to cap it all, the gravy's turned to gloop
and I didn't really want to serve
green bowls of thin sprout soup.

Science

Why does the sun go in at night?
Why does the sky go dim?
And why does the moon have a pull on the sea
making it rush out and in?

That Eureka moment meant nothing to me
when old Archimedes yelled 'Hey –
when I sit in the tub all the water spills out.
The world will be grateful, one day.'

And then there's combustion, to me that means spark.
It's what makes my car engine go.
I pump in the petrol, exhaust fumes puff out –
that's much more than I need to know.

But what of the atom, and why did it split?
Who knows? And who cares? What's it worth?
In the great scheme of things one split atom is small –
but what is its impact on Earth?

Man has been to the moon, flown in space, mined Earth's core.
Man has transplanted organs galore.
Made babies in test tubes, cloned sheep, cured the pox . . .
but we haven't fed Africa's poor.

So science is progress, they like us to think,
those men in their labs of that ilk.
And nothing is sacred, or so it would seem,
now our cows can give ready-skimmed milk!

Lonely hearts

Of course the heart is lonely, it lives all by itself
inside the body's cavity, it sits there on the shelf.
While lungs and kidneys come in pairs and brain in left and
right
and arms and legs and hands and feet have met their match for
life,
the poor old heart beats all alone, no romance makes him
quiver.
He yearns that one day, hopes it's soon, he'll meet Miss Lonely
Liver!

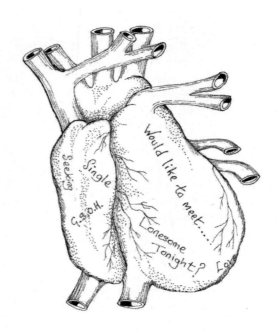

Laughter

I used to enjoy having a laugh,
the sort that makes you cry until it hurts,
until you find it impossible to breathe
and your nose is running and you think
I don't even know why I'm laughing.

And don't you feel good when it stops?
Relaxed all over, and tired too,
in the way you do after a swim
or a run, or cycling, or sex.

And you don't even mind what you look like.
Besides, you're too weak to care
that your face is screwed up, streaked with make-up
and your mouth's hanging open with your fillings on show.

Oh no. That reminds me.
I don't do laughter any more,
not since Saturday, chewing a toffee, and four of my teeth fell
   out.

On no, laughter's not for me. These days
I keep my lips sealed, my head down,
shy Diana smile, concealed by my hand.
If I remember.

So excuse me if I don't join in wholehearted
with your mirth and merriment, at least until next year.
'After Christmas,' the dentist said, 'can't get it done before. Too
   busy.'

And if I should forget and open wide and bellow with hilarity,
displaying toothless gums and stumps,
please don't mistake me for a Halloween witch
and send me packing
on my broomstick.

The missing member

'It's time to start,' the chairman said and closed the bottom bar
   door.
'Or should we wait for Jonathan? Give him a minute more?'

'No we should start without him,' replied the chairman's chum.
'He's had time to get here – I don't think he will come.
'If we begin without him it would be for the best
'then he'll have to sit down quietly and not be such a pest.

'Oh yes,' piped up the blonde one as she downed another drink
'I like it best when he's not here; it gives me time to think.'

The engineer sat on the fence; he knew not what to say.
He really couldn't stand the man; he hoped he'd gone away.
And then the drama teacher, a gentle soul at heart,
surprised them all with waspish words 'He never plays his
   part.'

A late arrival stumbled in. The others paid no heed.
She had her mind on other things, especially smoking weed.

'I've had enough of you lot. You're being so unfair,'
The ex-cop put her coffee
   down and stood up from
   her chair.
'No wonder he's gone
   missing, you make him
   feel a twerp.'
She picked her coffee up
   again and had another
   slurp.

'Nefi blw' the Welsh one
   cried, 'I've had enough of
   this.
Why don't we just phone
   up his wife and ask her
   where he is?'

The clock struck 14

'The clock just struck 14,' I said,
'it must be going wrong.'
He looked at me with puzzled brow
and said 'But not for long.'
He took an axe and chopped it down
– it made a mighty crash –
and shoved it on the bonfire,
just adding to the stash.
'You can't do that,' I shouted out.
'Too late,' was his reply,
'I've done it now, it was no good,
it had to go, that's why
I've chopped it up. It's now a pyre
for you to go upon'.
He said no more but took the axe
to me. My poem's done!

also by Jackie Williamson

Writing Letters and Reports for Thames Valley Police *(textbook)*

Banbury *(anthology) Published by Ottakar's*

In Her Element *(anthology) Published by Honno*

Cevamp, Mike and Me *Published by Acorns Publishing*

Editor: Best Friends – the story of Dogs for the Disabled *to be published Summer 2009*

Coming soon: Whale Steak and Chips – an elderly widow relects on her childhood, teen years, married life and old age.